Answers

Section One — The Design Process

Page 4 — Design Briefs

1 a) E.g. Design a storage system with enough compartments to hold all the plumber's tools so that they don't get mixed up *[1 mark for any suitable answer]*.

b) E.g. Design a small toy or game suitable for children to use on a long car or train journey that will hold their attention *[1 mark for any suitable answer]*.

2 a) E.g. water pistols encourage children to play with each other / get fresh air / exercise *[1 mark]*.

b) E.g. it's morally irresponsible to encourage children to play with guns *[1 mark]*.

3 a) Market pull is when a new product is designed as a result of consumer demand / what consumers want *[1 mark]*.

b) *Technology push* — New technologies make new features or better designs possible *[1 mark]* e.g. touchscreen technology / colour screens / internet access / very small phones *[1 mark]*.
Market pull — e.g. people want to carry fewer devices *[1 mark]* so now phones have built-in cameras / diaries / music players / email access *[1 mark]*.

Page 5 — Product Analysis — 1

1 a) *Chair A* — e.g. dining room / home / church *[1 mark for any suitable answer]*.
Chair B — e.g. school / library / village hall *[1 mark for any suitable answer]*.

b) i) E.g. aesthetic reasons / very durable *[1 mark for any suitable answer]*.

ii) E.g. cheap / can be produced in a range of colours *[1 mark for any suitable answer]*.

c) Chair B *[1 mark]*. E.g. they can be stacked easily / they're waterproof / they're lighter so they're easier to transport *[1 mark]*.

2 E.g. the length of the chair legs, size of the seat and the height of the back support are in the right proportions for the anthropometric data. This means the chair should give a comfortable sitting position for most males in this age range. But, the chair might be less comfortable for people who do not have these proportions or do not fall into this category, e.g. 18-40 females *[Total 3 marks — 1 mark for each valid point]*.

Page 6 — Product Analysis — 2

3 a) E.g. both whisks look like they'll do the job they're intended for *[1 mark]* but the electric whisk will be quicker / require less effort *[1 mark]*.

b) *Hand whisk* — e.g. it does not use electricity / it is made from fewer parts / it has undergone fewer processes during its manufacture / no moving parts mean it is less likely to break and need replacing / made from metal which can be recycled *[2 marks — 1 for each suitable point]*.
Electric whisk — e.g. requires electricity to work / a lot of stages needed to manufacture / parts made from plastic which is unlikely to have come from renewable sources / difficult to recycle *[2 marks — 1 for each suitable point]*.

4 *Product A* — e.g. product A doesn't require batteries which means it can't run out of power on the camping trip / torch design makes it easy to carry / tough plastic means the product won't be damaged easily *[2 marks — 1 for each suitable point]*.
Product B provides light to a wide area / the batteries might run out and couldn't be recharged on the camping trip *[2 marks — 1 for each suitable point]*.

Page 7 — Research and Design Specification — 1

1 a) E.g. the points are too vague / don't provide specific information / are not quantified *[1 mark]*.

b) *Point 1* — the rack should fit on a shelf that is 200 mm deep *[1 mark for specifying a sensible size of a shelf]*.
Point 2 — the rack must be silver coloured *[1 mark for specifying a finish or colour]*.
Point 3 — the rack must hold 20 CDs *[1 mark for specifying the number of CDs to be stored]*.

2 a) E.g. a children's bookcase may be more colourful / have no sharp corners for safety / be shorter with lower shelves / have a non-toxic finish *[3 marks — 1 for each suitable answer]*.

b) E.g. bookcase must include primary colours / should have rounded corners / bookcase must not be more than 700 mm high (any suitable size) / the bookcase should be made from plastic *[3 marks — 1 for each suitable point]*.

Page 8 — Research and Design Specification — 2

3 a) E.g. to understand what potential customers want / to work out how many people might buy your product *[1 mark for any suitable answer]*.

b) E.g. the toast rack should hold at least two slices of bread *[1 mark]*. The toast rack should have gaps big enough to hold thick cut toast *[1 mark]*. The rack should be made from aluminium *[1 mark]*.

4 E.g. it must be durable — it will be used for many years. / It must be weatherproof — it will be outside. / It must be stable — so it doesn't fall over or collapse during use. / It must be ergonomically designed — suitable size for use by children. / It should be safe to use — children shouldn't hurt themselves whilst sitting on the swing. *[6 marks — 1 mark for each reason, 1 mark for each explanation]*

Page 9 — Generating Proposals

1
- fulfilling all the requirements of the design brief *[2 marks]*, fulfilling all but one requirement of the design brief *[1 mark]*
- creating a creative, original idea *[1 mark]*
E.g. 'carrot'-shaped hutch

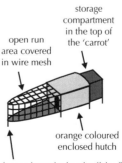

Answers

2 Total 6 marks:
- up to 2 marks for each idea.
- creative, original idea *[2 marks]*
- simple obvious idea *[1 mark]*
- idea closely resembles one of the other ideas *[0 marks]*

E.g. boy's bed — dinosaur bed

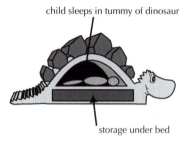

Page 10 — Development — 1

1 a) E.g. able to test the product / identify problems / save money by identifying problems at early stage / can ask potential customers their opinions / easy to make changes to the design at this early stage *[2 marks — 1 for each point]*.

b) *Material* — e.g. card / modelling clay / high-density polystyrene foam / jellutong.
Reason — e.g. cheap / easy to work / quick to produce a model *[2 marks — 1 mark for material, 1 mark for reason]*.

c) E.g. they could be painted on with a stencil *[1 mark]*.

d) E.g.
Change — remove fabric flag.
Explanation — makes the construction easier by reducing the number of different materials.
Change — remove string rigging.
Explanation — makes the construction easier by reducing the number of different materials.
Change — combine the three hull pieces and the funnels into one piece.
Explanation — makes the construction easier if all in one piece because you don't need to fix them together.
[4 marks — 1 mark for each suitable change, 1 mark for explanation of change]

Page 11 — Development — 2

2 a) E.g. the design has enough room to store 20 DVD boxes. / The design would be able to fit on a shelf and is free-standing. / The idea would show the spines of the DVD boxes. / The idea doesn't use curves and flowing lines *[4 marks — 1 for each statement]*.

b) E.g.

Total 15 marks:
- meeting the specification
  design meets all the specification points *[2 marks]*
  design meets some of the specification points *[1 mark]*
- sketching
  3D sketch that is rendered *[3 marks]*
  3D sketch *[2 marks]*
  line sketch *[1 mark]*
- notes
  explanation of design features *[2 marks]*
  only using labels *[1 mark]*
- specifying materials
  all specific materials given *[3 marks]*
  some specific materials given *[2 marks]*
  general materials given *[1 mark]*
- important sizes
  all realistic dimensions given *[2 marks]*
  only one realistic dimension given *[1 mark]*
- constructional details
  enough detail that someone else could make the product *[3 marks]*
  most detail given *[2 marks]*
  some detail given *[1 mark]*

Page 12 — Designing Safe Products

1 a) E.g. ridged edge gives better grip so it doesn't slip out the hand / the blade can lock in position so it doesn't move when cutting / the blade is retractable so it can go back in the knife when not being used *[2 marks — 1 mark for each point]*.

b) i) The product meets the requirements of the relevant standards in the European Union (EU) *[1 mark]*.

ii) The product meets the standards of the British Standards Institution (BSI) *[1 mark]*.

2 E.g. no small parts which could cause choking / no small holes which could trap fingers / no sharp edges that could cause injuries / paints must be non-toxic, etc. *[3 marks — 1 for each requirement]*

3 a) E.g. 'wood guaranteed against rot for 10 years' / 'the shed will hold 4 adult bikes', 'all wood comes from a sustainable source', 'guaranteed fully waterproof for life' *[3 marks — 1 for each sensible claim]*

b) Any claims made about the product must be accurate in order to comply with laws such as the Trade Descriptions Act *[1 mark]*.

Page 13 — Drawing Techniques — 1

1 Third angle orthographic projection *[1 mark]*.

2 a)

[1 mark]

b)

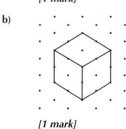

[1 mark]

CGP

GCSE D&T
Resistant Materials

AQA Specification

Answer Book

Contents

Section One — The Design Process 3
Section Two — Tools and Processes 6
Section Three — Materials and Components 9
Section Four — Systems 11
Section Five — Safety and the Environment 12
Section Six — Industrial Awareness 14

Published by Coordination Group Publications Ltd
ISBN: 978 1 84762 398 0
www.cgpbooks.co.uk
Printed by Elanders Ltd, Newcastle upon Tyne.

Based on the classic CGP style created by Richard Parsons.

Text, design, layout and original illustrations © Coordination Group Publications Ltd. 2009
All rights reserved.

Answers

3 Total 2 marks:
- showing shelves and side panels moved apart *[1 mark]*
- using dotted lines to show where the parts have come from *[1 mark]*

Page 14 — Drawing Techniques — 2

4 *Wooden block* — brown with grain shown *[1 mark]*
Plastic block — flat tone with light highlights *[1 mark]*
Concrete block — grey with rough textured parts *[1 mark]*

5

z axis, y axis, x axis

[1 mark]

6

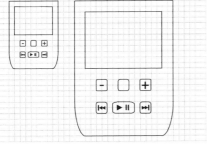

[1 mark for correct scaling of image, 1 mark for correct shape of image, 1 mark for quality of drawing (e.g. ruler used)]

Page 15 — Drawing Techniques — 3

7 a) millimetres *[1 mark]*
b) Total 6 marks:
- correct drawing of front view *[1 mark]*
- correct drawing of end view *[1 mark]*
- using solid thick outlines *[1 mark]*
- correct use of construction lines *[1 mark]*
- correct use of centre lines *[1 mark]*
- correctly adding dimension lines *[1 mark]*

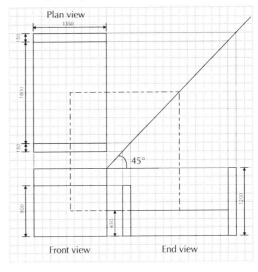

Page 16 — Planning for Manufacture — 1

1 a) To make sure components and products are good quality / meet the manufacturing specification *[1 mark]*.
b) E.g. check the surfaces are smooth — after edges and surfaces have been sanded / check the paint has been applied evenly — after undercoat has been applied to parts / check the paint has been applied evenly — after topcoat has been applied / check unit is assembled correctly — after the unit has been assembled *[Total 4 marks — 1 for each quality control check, 1 mark for identifying when each check should happen]*.

2 a) No *[1 mark]* — that level of accuracy isn't needed for the string length *[1 mark]*.
b) No *[1 mark]* — if the hole is 5 mm the knot will probably fall through / if the hole is 1 mm wide the string won't fit through *[1 mark]*.
c) Yes *[1 mark]* — that amount of accuracy is sensible for cutting round the shape / it doesn't matter if one sheep is a few mm taller than another *[1 mark]*.

Answers

Page 17 — Planning for Manufacture — 2

3   Total 6 marks:
- including each stage *[up to 4 marks — 1 mark for each stage]*
- including a suitable quality control check and feedback loop e.g. are dimensions correct / are edges smooth / is glue set etc. *[1 mark]*
- putting all stages in a sensible order *[1 mark]*

E.g.

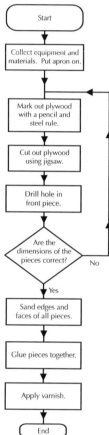

Section Two — Tools and Processes

Page 18 — Hand and Power Tools — 1

1 a)   Try square *[1 mark]*
   b)   E.g.

Process	Hand tool
Cut the piece of wood to size.	Ripsaw / tenon saw
Make pilot holes for the hanging holes.	Bradawl
Make the hanging holes.	Hand drill / brace
Angle the edges on the front face.	Bench plane

[1 mark for each correct answer]

2 a)   i)   Flat bit *[1 mark]*
     ii)   Countersink bit *[1 mark]*
   b)   Coping saw / jigsaw *[1 mark]* as it can be used to cut curves in wood *[1 mark]*.

Page 19 — Hand and Power Tools — 2

3 a)   *Name* — jigsaw *[1 mark]*
      Process — making straight and curved cuts in wood, metal or plastic *[1 mark]*
   b)   *Name* — circular saw *[1 mark]*
      Process — making straight cuts in wood *[1 mark]*
   c)   *Name* — hand/flat file *[1 mark]*
      Process — removal of material from / finishing metals, plastics or wood *[1 mark]*
   d)   *Name* — cold chisel / chisel *[1 mark]*
      Process — cut away / shape metal *[1 mark]*
   e)   *Name* — bench plane *[1 mark]*
      Process — shaving off thin layers of wood *[1 mark]*

Page 20 — Machine Tools

1 a)   band saw *[1 mark]*
   b)   lathe *[1 mark]*
   c)   bench grinder *[1 mark]*

2   *Machine tool* — e.g. a pillar drill / pedestal drill *[1 mark]*.
     Safety precautions — e.g. put goggles on / ensure safety guards on machine are in place / tie hair back / tuck clothes in / remove chuck key / locate emergency stop button / ensure piece of steel is securely clamped *[1 mark]*.

3   Cut metal to 140 mm using band saw *[1 mark]*. Turn down to 50 mm diameter on lathe *[1 mark]*. Turn down one end to 25 mm diameter and to a length of 60 mm *[1 mark]*.

Page 21 — Forming and Bending — 1

1 a)   E.g. iron / steel *[1 mark]*.
   b)   The metal is first heated up in a forge *[1 mark]*. When the metal is hot and has softened, it is hammered into shape on the anvil *[1 mark]*.

2 a)   Heat it slowly *[1 mark]* and allow it to cool *[1 mark]*.
   b)   • Diagram showing metal in a bending jig/vice *[1 mark]*.
       • Labelled and annotated correctly *[1 mark]*.
       E.g.

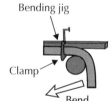

Page 22 — Forming and Bending — 2

3 a)   line bender / strip heater *[1 mark]*
   b)   The sheet of plastic is positioned on top of the line bender/strip heater so that the heating element is directly below the line to be bent *[1 mark]*. This softens the plastic and it can be bent into shape *[1 mark]*.

4 a)   Laminating is gluing thin strips or sheets of a material, e.g. wood, together *[1 mark]*.
   b)   Diagram and notes covering:
- glue applied to two (or more) thin wood strips *[1 mark]*.
- wood strips then bent into correct shape using a jig *[1 mark]*.
- wood strips held in the jig until glue dries *[1 mark]*.

Answers

E.g.

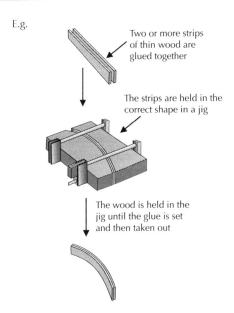

Page 23 — Casting and Moulding — 1

1. Diagram and notes covering:
   - Tube of softened plastic inserted into bottle-shaped mould *[1 mark]*.
   - Air being blown in *[1 mark]*.
   - Plastic taking shape of mould *[1 mark]*.

   E.g.

   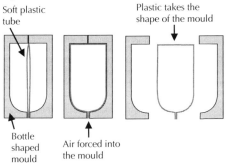

2. a) die casting *[1 mark]*
   b) extrusion *[1 mark]*
   c) press moulding / injection moulding / vacuum forming *[1 mark]*

3. - Diagram showing granules of plastic/metal being heated up *[1 marks]*.
   - Diagram showing pressure used *[1 mark]* to force molten plastic/metal through a mould *[1 mark]*.
   - Appropriate notes describing the process *[1 mark]*.

   E.g.

   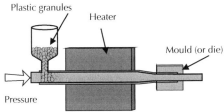

   The heater melts the plastic granules.
   The plastic is then forced through the mould using high pressure.
   The shape of the plastic extruded is the same as the exit hole of the mould.

Page 24 — Casting and Moulding — 2

4. a) *Manufacturing process* — Die casting *[1 mark]*.
   Description — Molten metal *[1 mark]* is poured into a mould/die *[1 mark]*. The metal sets and the mould is removed to give the product *[1 mark]*.
   b) *Manufacturing process* — Vacuum forming *[1 mark]*
   Description — A sheet of thermoplastic is heated until it goes soft *[1 mark]* over a mould which is put on a vacuum bed *[1 mark]*. The air is sucked out from underneath the plastic to make a vacuum and the pressure forces the plastic over the mould *[1 mark]*.
   c) *Manufacturing process* — Injection moulding *[1 mark]*
   Description — Plastic granules are melted *[1 mark]*. The liquid plastic is forced into a mould/die under pressure *[1 mark]*. The plastic sets and the mould is removed *[1 mark]*.

Page 25 — Assembly and Finishing

1. a) A 'dry-run' is assembling a product without glue *[1 mark]*. The drawer should be built without glue first to check that all the parts fit together *[1 mark]*.
   b) i) The drawer pieces should be painted before they're fitted together *[1 mark]*. This will make the painting process easier / avoid paints ending up on the wrong parts of the drawer *[1 mark]*.
   ii) 1. The surface of the wood should be smoothed with e.g. glass paper *[1 mark]*.
   2. The surface should be cleaned / surface dust removed *[1 mark]*.

Page 26 — Screws, Bolts and Nails

1. a) (left) slotted *[1 mark]* countersunk screw *[1 mark]*
   (right) crossed *[1 mark]* roundhead screw *[1 mark]*
   b) A screw that cut its own threaded holes (in metals and hard plastics) *[1 mark]*.
   c) wood *[1 mark]*
   d) *Bolt* —
   - Diagram showing a bolt *[1 mark]* with a square/hexagonal head *[1 mark]*.
   - Correctly labelled thread and shank *[1 mark]*.

   E.g.

   Machine screw to be tightened with an Allen key —
   - Diagram showing machine screw *[1 mark]* with hexagonal shaped hole in head for Allen key *[1 mark]*.
   - Correctly labelled thread and shank *[1 mark]*.

   E.g.

2. Diagram and notes showing:
   - split die *[1 mark]* and die holder *[1 mark]*.
   - split die rotated around rod to cut the thread *[1 mark]*

   E.g.

   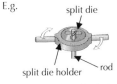

   When the split die holder is rotated it cuts the thread into the rod

Answers

Page 27 — Joints — 1

1

Joint	Name	Product
	Mitred joint	E.g. Picture frames
	Dowel joint	E.g. Factory-made furniture such as tables
	Housing joint	E.g. Drawer bottoms / shelves
	Dovetail joint	E.g. Decorative purposes / drawers
	Butt joint	E.g. Cheap furniture such as shoe racks
	Halving joint	E.g. Frame construction for cabinets
	Lap joint	E.g. Boxes / drawers
	Mortise and tenon joint	E.g. Tables and Chairs

[1 mark for each name, 1 mark for each sensible product]

Page 28 — Joints — 2

2 a) E.g. Contact adhesive / epoxy resin *[1 mark]*
 b) E.g. PVA / contact adhesive / epoxy resin *[1 mark]*
3 a) Joint — knock-down joint *[1 mark]*
   Reason — easy to take apart and re-join *[1 mark]*
 b) Joint — housing joint *[1 mark]*
   Reason — supports weight well / good surface area for gluing *[1 mark]*
 c) Joint — dovetail joint *[1 mark]*
   Reason — looks attractive/decorative *[1 mark]*
 d) Joint — mortise and tenon joint *[1 mark]*
   Reason — strong *[1 mark]*

Page 29 — Joining Metals — 1

1 a) Thoroughly clean/degrease the metals with a solvent such as white spirit *[1 mark]*. Apply flux (to stop air from oxidising the metal during heating) *[1 mark]*.
 b) A gas brazing torch/blow torch/electric-arc welder is used to heat the joint *[1 mark]*. When the metal is hot enough, spelter is applied into the joint *[1 mark]*.
 c) E.g. welding is stronger than brazing *[1 mark]*.
2 a) Diagrams and notes showing:
   - metal pin being inserted through a pop rivet *[1 mark]*
   - rivet and pin in hole of sheet material *[1 mark]*
   - riveter being used to pull and snap off the pin leaving rivet expanded on the 'blind' side *[1 mark]*
   - Labelled and annotated correctly *[1 mark]*
 b) E.g. quicker / easier / safer than welding or brazing / only need access to one side of the metal *[1 mark each, up to 2 marks]*

Page 30 — Joining Metals — 2

3 a) The metal is greasy *[1 mark]* and the two pieces do not fit together well *[1 mark]*.
 b) Metal is heated up to a very high temperature *[1 mark]* using an oxyacetylene torch/electric-arc welder/laser *[1 mark]*. This melts the two pieces of metal so the edges flow together *[1 mark]*.
 c) E.g. welding mask, visor / overalls / heat-proof gloves / heavy-duty boots or shoes *[2 marks — 1 for each answer]*.
4 a) Solder is heated up using a soldering iron or a blow torch *[1 mark]*. The molten solder flows between the two metals and cools and solidifies to form the joint *[1 mark]*.
 b) Brazing/welding *[1 mark]*.

Page 31 — CAD/CAM

1 *Advantages* — E.g. makes design processes easier — developing and editing 2D and 3D images of designs, viewing 3D designs from all angles. / It's easy to experiment with different materials and finishes. / CAD can be used to produce final presentation drawings to show clients. / Products can be machined at high speed. / Machines can run 24 hours a day. / Machines can work in hazardous conditions. / CAM gives a high quality finish. / There is no human error in CAM. / Labour costs are lower. *[1 mark for each correct advantage, up to 3 marks]*
 Disadvantages — E.g. computers can get viruses/software problems/corrupted files that can slow down production. / Initial investment in equipment/training is high. / Workers may have to be made redundant, leading to poor morale. *[1 mark]*
2 First stage —
   - name the equipment used to control the computer, e.g. keyboard / mouse / graphics tablet *[1 mark]*
   - name the CAD software that could be used to produce the design, e.g. SolidWorks® / Pro/DESKTOP® *[1 mark]*
   - details of how the design is produced using the software *[1 mark for a basic description, 2 marks for a clear, detailed description]*
   Second stage —
   - state that the CAD data is transferred to a CAM machine *[1 mark]*
   - name the additive / subtractive CAM machine that you would use, e.g. milling machine / CNC router *[1 mark]*
   - details of how the CAM machine will shape the component *[1 mark for a basic description, 2 marks for a clear, detailed description]*

Page 32 — Quality Assurance and Control — 1

1 a) E.g. to make sure that the products conform to the manufacturing specification / do the job they're supposed to do / meet the standards set by standards institutions / keep the customers happy / are manufactured consistently *[1 mark each, up to 3 marks]*.
 b) E.g. it could be tested to see if the joints are tight / if the legs match / if it stands level / if it has a smooth finish / if its measurements are within tolerances / if it can support the weight it should *[1 mark each, up to 2 marks]*.
 c) E.g. good staff training procedures / systems for keeping machinery maintained *[1 mark]*.

Answers

2 a) Upper limit — 51 mm *[1 mark]*
   Lower limit — 49 mm *[1 mark]*
b) limit gauge *[1 mark]*
c) E.g. it is faster *[1 mark]*

Page 33 — Quality Assurance and Control — 2

3 a) E.g. check that the materials match the design specification / are of high quality / check tools are sharp *[1 mark]*.
b) E.g. check marking out is accurate / check sizes of pieces are within tolerances *[1 mark]*.
c) E.g. check that CDs fit into the rack / check that the finish is smooth / check the construction is solid *[1 mark each, up to 2 marks]*.
4 a) It can be used to check the welding for cracks *[1 mark]*.
b) It can be used to check that the weight the blade can carry matches the design specification *[1 mark]*.
c) It can be used to check, e.g. that the logo is printed correctly / the varnish is smooth *[1 mark]*.

Section Three — Materials and Components

Page 34 — Properties of Materials

1 a) Material — e.g. acrylic / high density polyethylene (HDPE) *[1 mark]*.
   Property — e.g. durable / easy to mould into different designs *[1 mark]*.
b) Material — e.g. teak / mahogany / pine *[1 mark]*.
   Property — e.g. durable / heavy so it won't be blown over / wood grain looks attractive. *[1 mark]*.
2 a) Property — hardness *[1 mark]*.
   Explanation — it needs to be hard so that it doesn't wear with use *[1 mark]*.
b) Property — strength *[1 mark]*.
   Explanation — it needs to be strong enough to cope with the weight that is put on it *[1 mark]*.
c) Property — toughness *[1 mark]*.
   Explanation — it needs to be able to absorb an impact *[1 mark]*.

Page 35 — Metals — 1

1 a) Ferrous means a metal contains iron *[1 mark]*.
b) Check if the metal is magnetic *[1 mark]*.
2 E.g. steel — iron and carbon / brass — copper and zinc. *[1 mark for naming an alloy, 1 mark for naming the metals that make that alloy]*
3 a) Sheet metal *[1 mark]*.
b) Tubular metal / pipe *[1 mark]*.
c) I shaped girder *[1 mark]*.
4 a) Warm the metal until it is red hot and then plunge it into cold water or oil *[1 mark]*. This process makes the metal harder, but also more brittle *[1 mark]*.
b) To temper metal you first clean it and then gently warm it *[1 mark]*. Tempering makes the metal tougher and less brittle *[1 mark]*.

Page 36 — Metals — 2

5 a) Name — e.g. aluminium *[1 mark]*.
   Reason — e.g. lightweight / corrosion resistant *[1 mark]*.
b) Name — e.g. brass *[1 mark]*.
   Reason — e.g. strong / malleable / looks attractive *[1 mark]*.
c) Name — e.g. copper *[1 mark]*.
   Reason — e.g. soft / malleable *[1 mark]*.

6

Type of Steel	Hardness	Resistance to Corrosion	Product
Mild Steel	relatively soft	poor - rusts easily	nails
High-carbon Steel	fairly hard	fair - will rust slowly	e.g. drills / files / chisels / saws
Stainless Steel	very hard	very good - won't rust	e.g. medical equipment / sinks / kettles / cutlery

[5 marks — 1 mark for each answer in the table]

Page 37 — Metals — 3

7 a) Protection (from abrasion / corrosion) *[1 mark]*.
b) i) E.g. a radiator *[1 mark]*. Apply a primer first so that the paint can form a good bond. Allow the primer to dry and then apply one or more coats of paint *[1 mark]*
   ii) E.g. a chrome bumper *[1 mark]*. This can be done by hand / using a buffing wheel *[1 mark]*.
   iii) E.g. a brass door handle / brass instruments *[1 mark]*. Apply a thin layer of cellulose / gum / varnish *[1 mark]*.
   iv) E.g. wire dishwasher drawer *[1 mark]*. The metal is heated evenly and then dipped into fluidised powder to apply a thin layer of plastic. (It is then returned to the oven to fuse the plastic to the metallic surface) *[1 mark]*.
8 a) Iron is mined *[1 mark]* as iron ore. The ore is crushed and heated with other materials in a blast furnace to separate the metal out *[1 mark]*. Molten iron is taken from the furnace and cooled to make blocks *[1 mark]*.
b) Any two from e.g. mining disfigures the landscape / processing and refining metals causes pollution / transporting the ore and metal causes pollution / metal is dumped in landfill sites *[2 marks — 1 for each answer]*.

Page 38 — Plastics — 1

1 a) Plastic — e.g. polyethylene *[1 mark]*.
   Type — thermoplastic *[1 mark]*.
   Reason — e.g. flexible so bottle is squeezable *[1 mark]*.
b) Plastic — e.g. urea-formaldehyde *[1 mark]*.
   Type — thermosetting plastic *[1 mark]*.
   Reason — good electrical insulator *[1 mark]*.
c) Plastic — e.g. melamine-formaldehyde *[1 mark]*.
   Type — thermosetting plastic *[1 mark]*.
   Reason — good thermal insulator *[1 mark]*.
d) Plastic — e.g. acrylic *[1 mark]*.
   Type — thermoplastic *[1 mark]*.
   Reason — very durable outdoors *[1 mark]*.

Page 39 — Plastics — 2

2 a) Producing — e.g. turning crude oil into plastic requires a lot of energy which is likely to come from burning fossil fuels / produces a lot of pollution / uses up reserves of crude oil which is a finite resource *[1 mark]*.
   Disposing — e.g. the plastics are often disposed of into landfill sites *[1 mark]*.

Answers

b) E.g. the plastic needs to be sorted by hand which means paying labour costs *[1 mark]*. The recycling of plastics also uses a lot of energy which costs money *[1 mark]*.

3 a) E.g. it is lightweight which means that it doesn't contribute much to the weight of the product and packaging / it is cushioning which means it can help absorb impacts and protect the product *[1 mark]*.

b) E.g. it is naturally resistant to corrosion and decay *[1 mark]*.

c) Thermoplastics can be re-melted easily *[1 mark]* allowing them to be reformed and used again *[1 mark]*. Thermosetting plastics are chemically changed when they are heated *[1 mark]* and cannot be melted and re-moulded afterwards so they cannot be recycled *[1 mark]*.

Page 40 — Wood and Boards — 1

1 a) Name — e.g. chipboard *[1 mark]*.
Reason — it is a cheap material which makes it suitable for mass produced flat pack furniture *[1 mark]*.

b) Name — e.g. MDF *[1 mark]*.
Reason — it has a smooth surface so it's easy to paint *[1 mark]*.

2 a) Name — e.g. beech *[1 mark]*.
Reason — e.g. beech gives a durable surface to work on / it is pleasing to look at (aesthetic) / it is quite a cheap material *[2 marks — 1 for each point]*.

b) Name — e.g. oak *[1 mark]*.
Reason — e.g. oak is very strong / it is long lasting / it creates a desirable, traditional look *[2 marks — 1 for each point]*.

Page 41 — Wood and Boards — 2

3 a) Trees can be replanted to replace the wood that is used *[1 mark]*.

b) It means that something will decay over time *[1 mark]*.

c) E.g. Low quality wood can be recycled by chipping or shredding it *[1 mark]*. It can be used to make chip board / compost *[1 mark]*.

d) They contain glue which is hard to separate out *[1 mark]*.

4 a) Finish — e.g. polyurethane paint *[1 mark]*.
Reason — e.g. tough / waterproof *[1 mark]*.

b) Finish — e.g. polyurethane varnish *[1 mark]*.
Reason — e.g. protects the wood / wood's appearance is enhanced, not covered *[1 mark]*.

Page 42 — Composites and New Materials — 1

1 a) A composite material is one that is formed by bonding two or more materials together *[1 mark]*.

b) E.g.
  i) Glass-reinforced plastic (GRP) *[1 mark]*
  ii) Product — Boats *[1 mark]*
  Explanation — GRP is lightweight, but stronger than normal plastic which makes it a good material to make boat hulls from *[1 mark]*.

2 a) A smart material is a material that changes its properties when the environment changes *[1 mark]*.

b) i) Thermochromic ink *[1 mark]*
  ii) The colour change could be used to tell the user when the pan is hot enough to cook in *[1 mark]* or to warn the user that the pan is too hot to touch *[1 mark]*.

  iii) E.g. colour-changing feeding spoon for babies to warn parents if food is too hot *[1 mark]*.

c) E.g. polymorph *[1 mark]*

Page 43 — Composites and New Materials — 2

3 a) 'Self-cleaning' glass can be made by coating it in a layer of nanoparticles *[1 mark]* which break down surface dirt so that it is easily washed away by rain *[1 mark]*.

b) Advantage — e.g. nanocomposite plastics can be made stronger and lighter than ordinary plastics *[1 mark]*.
Disadvantage — e.g. nanocomposite plastics are more expensive than ordinary plastics *[1 mark]*.

c) E.g. there may be long term health problems resulting from exposure to nanomaterials that we don't yet know about / Nanoparticles are very small and light, so could be carried in the air easily and contaminate the atmosphere *[1 mark for any sensible concern]*.

4 E.g.
Nitinol could be used to make the frames of the glasses *[1 mark]*. Nitinol is a shape memory alloy — if you deform products made from it, they can be returned to their original shape by heating *[1 mark]* so glasses made from nitinol can be easily fixed if they get accidentally bent out of shape *[1 mark]*.
Photochromic glass could be used for the lenses *[1 mark]*. Photochromic materials change colour when exposed to different levels of light *[1 mark]* so sunglasses with photochromic lenses can be designed to get darker in bright light, and clearer in low light *[1 mark]*.

Page 44 — Fixtures and Fittings

1 a) 3 marks in total:
- correct type of hinge sketched *[1 mark]*
- clear and accurate sketch *[1 mark]*
- sensible advantage identified *[1 mark]*

E.g.

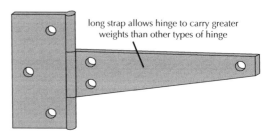

long strap allows hinge to carry greater weights than other types of hinge

b) 3 marks in total:
- correct type of catch sketched *[1 mark]*
- clear and accurate sketch *[1 mark]*
- sensible advantage identified *[1 mark]*

E.g.

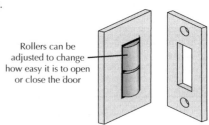

Rollers can be adjusted to change how easy it is to open or close the door

Answers

2 a) 8 marks in total:
- sketch of suitable hinge, e.g. flush hinge *[1 mark]*
- tools required for fitting hinge named *[1 mark]*
- notes / sketches showing how to attach hinges *[2 marks for detailed description that could be used by a third party or 1 mark for a basic description]*
- sketch of suitable locking mechanism *[1 mark]*
- tools required for fitting lock *[1 mark]*
- notes / sketches showing how to attach lock *[2 marks for detailed description that could be used by a third party or 1 mark for a basic description]*

E.g. fit two flush hinges and a surface lock to the cabinet door, positioned as shown:

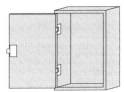

Fitting the lock to the door:
- Make a hole in the door, using a hand or pillar drill, of the correct size to hold the barrel of the lock.
- To fix the lock in place, use a bradawl to make pilot holes, then screw the lock in place with wood screws.

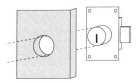

- When the lock is in place, mark out and cut a hole for the bolt using a wood chisel.

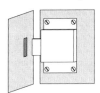

Finally, fit the hinges and attach door:
- Attach the smaller part of the hinge to the door, then attach the larger part to the side of the cabinet.
- Again, use a bradawl to make pilot holes, and screw the hinge in place using wood screws.

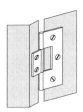

Page 45 — Adhesives

1 a) *Advantage* — e.g. forms a very strong bond *[1 mark]*
Disadvantage — e.g. can give off harmful fumes which means the area they are used in needs to be well-ventilated *[1 mark]*
Use — e.g. sticking down floor tiles *[1 mark]*

b) *Advantage* — e.g. forms very permanent bond / suitable for use in various medical situations *[1 mark]*
Disadvantage — e.g. can give off harmful fumes / can take hours to set *[1 mark]*
Use — e.g. to stick artificial joints to bones *[1 mark]*

c) *Advantage* — e.g. inexpensive *[1 mark]*
Disadvantage — e.g. not waterproof *[1 mark]*
Use — e.g. gluing together wooden furniture *[1 mark]*

2 Make sure surfaces to be joined are clean *[1 mark]*. Mix equal amounts of the resin and hardener *[1 mark]*. Apply the mixed epoxy resin to the surface to be glued immediately after mixing *[1 mark]*. Clamp the two pieces of metal together until the resin has completely set *[1 mark]*.

Section Four — Systems

Page 46 — Electrical Systems

1 a) (top to bottom) output, input *[1 mark]*
b) It is a good conductor of electricity *[1 mark]*.
c) E.g. PVC *[1 mark]*, it is an electrical insulator *[1 mark]*.

2 a) Thermistor *[1 mark]* — it senses changes in temperature, so could switch the circuit on at certain temperatures *[1 mark]*.
b) Motor *[1 mark]* — it makes things move, so could open the vent *[1 mark]*.

Page 47 — Mechanical Systems — 1

1 *Reciprocating* — moving backwards and forwards in a straight line *[1 mark]*, e.g. a piston head / jigsaw *[1 mark]*
Oscillating — moving backwards and forwards in an arc *[1 mark]*, e.g. a swing / pendulum / metronome *[1 mark]*
Rotary — moving in a circle *[1 mark]*, e.g. a wheel / helicopter rotor / washing machine drum *[1 mark]*.

2 a) A gear train *[1 mark]*
b) Idler gear *[1 mark]*
c) Clockwise *[1 mark]* because the idler gear gets turned anticlockwise *[1 mark]*.
d) Slower *[1 mark]* because gear B is larger with more teeth than the driver gear so it'll take longer to make one complete turn *[1 mark]*.

Page 48 — Mechanical Systems — 2

3 a) 4 marks in total:
- drawing of a rack and pinion that would work *[1 mark]*
- pinion gear and rack labelled *[1 mark]*
- correct relative directions of motion shown on pinion gear and rack *[1 mark]*
- neat and accurate drawing *[1 mark]*

E.g.

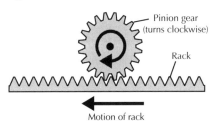

b) Rotary motion *[1 mark]* is turned into linear motion *[1 mark]*. (Marks also awarded if opposite order of motions given).

Answers

4 a) *Mechanism A* — bevel gears *[1 mark]*
Mechanism B — worm drive and worm wheel *[1 mark]*
b) *Similarity* — Both mechanisms change the direction of rotation through 90° / both transfer rotary motion from one component to another *[1 mark]*.
Difference — In Mechanism A both gears have many teeth and will turn at similar speeds, but in Mechanism B the worm drive only has one tooth meaning it will turn much faster than the worm wheel which has many teeth *[1 mark]*.

Page 49 — Mechanical Systems — 3

5 a) 4 marks in total:
- drawing of either mechanical system *[1 mark]*
- driver part and driven part of mechanism labelled *[1 mark]*
- correct relative directions of motion of driver and driven part of mechanism shown *[1 mark]*
- chain or belt labelled *[1 mark]*

b) *Belt drive* — e.g. cheap, especially if shafts are far apart / no lubrication needed *[1 mark]*
Chain and sprocket — e.g. toothed sprockets and chain mean the chain can't slip like a belt drive could / can handle much greater loads than a belt drive *[1 mark]*.

6 a) Pulley system B *[1 mark]*.
b) The two pulley arrangement shown only needs half the force to move it compared to Pulley system A *[1 mark]*.

Page 50 — Mechanical Systems — 4

7 a) Pear cam *[1 mark]*
b) The cam rotates making the follower move up and down *[1 mark]*. For half a turn (while the cam points in the opposite direction to that shown on the diagram) the follower will not move, then it will gently rise and fall *[1 mark]*, opening and closing the fuel intake valve *[1 mark]*.

8 a)
- Circular cam with off-centre pivot shown *[1 mark]*
- Cam, follower and movements labelled *[1 mark]*
E.g.

b) E.g. use a wheel follower / lubricate the cam *[1 mark]*
9 For each turn of the cam the follower will rise and suddenly fall *[1 mark]* four times *[1 mark]*.

Page 51 — Mechanical Systems — 5

10 a) top to bottom:
shaft, arm, handle *[1 mark]*
b) Make the arm longer *[1 mark]*.
11 a) The reciprocating motion of the slider (left-to-right in the diagram) *[1 mark]* is turned into rotary motion of the crank *[1 mark]*. (Marks also awarded if opposite order of motions given).
b) E.g. car engines *[1 mark]*.
12 a) a bell crank *[1 mark]*
b) It changes the direction of a force through 90° *[1 mark]*.

Page 52 — Mechanical Systems — 6

13 a) *Lever A* — a second class lever *[1 mark]*
Example — e.g. a wheelbarrow *[1 mark]*
Lever B — a first class lever *[1 mark]*
Example — e.g. a pair of scissors *[1 mark]*
b) They give a mechanical advantage meaning a large load can be moved with a small effort *[1 mark]*.
14 a) E.g.

[3 marks — 1 mark for each feature clearly shown]
b) E.g. shovel / boat paddle / cricket bat *[1 mark]*.

Section Five — Safety and the Environment

Page 53 — Social and Environmental Issues — 1

1 a) *Softwood* — e.g. pine / cedar / yew *[1 mark]*
Hardwood — e.g. oak / mahogany / beech / elm *[1 mark]*
b) Softwoods. Softwoods are usually from managed plantations where trees are replaced as quickly as they're felled *[1 mark]*. Hardwood trees often come from natural rainforests and are not replaced *[1 mark]*, so habitats are destroyed *[1 mark]*.
['Softwoods' with no explanation scores 0 marks.]

2 *Life span* — e.g. melamine-formaldehyde boxes would have a longer lifespan as it is a more durable material than cardboard *[1 mark]*.
Sustainability — e.g. using cardboard is more sustainable as it is recyclable, whereas melamine-formaldehyde cannot be recycled (because it is a thermosetting plastic) / using cardboard is more sustainable because cardboard is made from trees which are a sustainable resource, whereas plastics are made from oil, which is a finite resource *[1 mark]*.

3 *Human factor* — e.g. Workers should be protected *[1 mark]* from the dangers of working with hot plastic, such as risk of burns, dangerous fumes *[1 mark]*.
Financial factor — e.g. A new mould will have to be made in order to mass-produce the bottles *[1 mark]* — producing industrial moulds is expensive *[1 mark]*.
Environmental factor — e.g. Thermoplastics are recyclable *[1 mark]*, so the packaging company may consider making the bottles from recycled HDPE *[1 mark]*.

Page 54 — Social and Environmental Issues — 2

4 a) A sustainable product is one that doesn't use up finite resources *[1 mark]* or do lasting damage to the environment *[1 mark]*.
b) i) E.g. make the cup from a plastic which is easily recyclable *[1 mark]*, so the plastic can be reused even if the cup itself is only used once *[1 mark]*.
ii) E.g. make components easy and cheap to replace *[1 mark]* so that people will be more likely to repair the phone if it breaks, rather than throwing it away and buying a new one *[1 mark]*.

Answers

5 *2. Manufacture* — E.g. a drinks can is made from a single material so it will use fewer resources compared to a more complicated product like a glass bottle with a metal cap / generating the energy used to produce the cans may use up fossil fuels and create pollution *[1 mark]*.
3. Using the product — E.g. using a drinks can does not directly damage the environment / a can will only be used once before it needs to be disposed of *[1 mark]*.
4. Product disposal — E.g. the can could be a danger to wildlife if disposed of carelessly / aluminium drinks cans can be recycled instead of dumped in a landfill *[1 mark]*.

Page 55 — Social and Environmental Issues — 3

6 Any three sensible points, e.g.
- The coping saw does not use electricity *[1 mark]*. Electricity used to power the jigsaw may be generated by burning fossil fuels, which uses up finite resources and causes pollution *[1 mark]*.
- The coping saw has fewer parts / contains less material *[1 mark]*. More raw materials and more energy will be used up to manufacture all the parts of the jigsaw *[1 mark]*.
- Fewer processes are involved in the manufacture of the coping saw *[1 mark]*, so less energy is required to manufacture the coping saw *[1 mark]*.
- The wood used to make the handle of the coping saw is a renewable material *[1 mark]* (as more trees can be planted), whereas the jigsaw is made from metal and plastic, both of which are produced from finite resources *[1 mark]*.

7 *Repair*: E.g. make replacements available for mechanical parts *[1 mark]*.
Reuse: E.g. make the toy sturdy enough to last for many years so that it can be passed on to younger children *[1 mark]*.
Recycle: E.g. make the toy from materials that can be recycled, e.g. thermoplastics, aluminium *[1 mark]*.
Rethink: E.g. consider whether any moving parts could be powered by a wind-up mechanism rather than batteries *[1 mark]*.
Reduce: E.g. reduce the number of parts the toy is made from so that less energy and raw materials will be used up in its construction *[1 mark]*.
Refuse: E.g. try to make the toy energy efficient, as parents may be put off buying a battery powered toy that only has a short battery life *[1 mark]*.

Page 56 — Health and Safety — 1

1 a) *Name*: Goggles *[1 mark]*
Process: E.g. cutting wood with a circular saw, sanding using a grinding disc *[1 mark]*
b) *Name*: Face mask / dust mask *[1 mark]*
Process: E.g. spray painting *[1 mark]*
c) *Name*: Face shield *[1 mark]*
Process: E.g. welding *[1 mark]*

2 Any five sensible points, e.g.
- Long hair could get caught in the machinery, so should be tied back.
- Loose clothing could get caught in the machinery, so should be tucked in.
- Sawdust or cuttings could damage eyes, so safety glasses or goggles must be worn.
- Fingers could be cut by the blade when sawing, so hands should be kept well away from the blade at all times.
- Sawdust could be inhaled, so wear a dust mask and /or use a dust extractor.
- An exposed blade and pulley increases the risk of getting caught or cut, so close the guard and adjust it so the minimum length of blade needed is exposed.
- Risk of cutting fingers when removing cut pieces from blade, so cut pieces should be moved away from the blade using a push stick.

[1 mark for each point, up to a maximum of 5 marks]

Page 57 — Health and Safety — 2

3 a) Control of substances hazardous to health *[1 mark]*
b) E.g. acrylic cement *[1 mark]*
Any two precautions, e.g.
Use in a well ventilated area / keep away from heat sources and naked flames / wear eye protection
[2 marks — 1 for each point]

4 a) Any two precautions, e.g.
Tie back hair / tuck loose clothing in / wear safety glasses or goggles / wear dust mask / wear ear protection / keep power cable out of path of blade / keep hands well away from blade / use safety guard.
[2 marks — 1 for each point]
b) Any two precautions, e.g.
Tie back hair / tuck loose clothing in / wear safety glasses or goggles / wear dust mask / wear ear protection / wear protective gloves / keep guards in place / do not grind on side of wheel / hold chisel firmly. *[2 marks — 1 for each point]*
c) Any two precautions, e.g.
Don't touch tip of soldering iron / use in a well ventilated area / keep power cord away from tip of soldering iron / wash hands after handling solder / always put soldering iron back on its stand when not in use. *[2 marks — 1 for each point]*
d) Any two precautions, e.g.
Work in a well ventilated area / keep lacquer away from heat sources or naked flames / wear safety glasses or goggles / wear face mask.
[2 marks — 1 for each point]

Answers

Section Six — Industrial Awareness

Page 58 — Scale of Production

1 a) E.g. products are made to exactly meet a customer's requirements *[1 mark]*.
  b) E.g. They can take a long time to make / they require highly skilled labour / materials are not bought in bulk *[2 marks — 1 for each suitable point]*.
  c) E.g. hand-crafted pottery / original paintings / hand-made furniture *[1 mark for any suitable answer]*.
2 a) Production that goes for 24 hours a day without stopping at any point *[1 mark]*.
  b) *Advantage* — e.g. the process can be made very efficient / the cost per item is low *[1 mark for any suitable point]*.
  Disadvantage — e.g. it can only produce one product / it's expensive to set up *[1 mark for any suitable point]*.
3 a) *Batch production* — because the machines can be easily altered to produce the different types of bed frame *[1 mark for production type, 1 mark for the reason]*.
  b) *Mass production* — because it is a large order for one single product and mass production will be efficient *[1 mark for production type, 1 mark for the reason]*.

Page 59 — Manufacturing in Quantity — 1

1 a) E.g. each bathtub can be made more quickly / the machines are usually more efficient so they are cheaper to run / material can be bought in bulk *[2 marks — 1 mark for each reason]*.
  b) E.g. it would cost a lot to set up the factory / make new industrial moulds / buy new machinery / employ and train lots of staff *[2 marks — 1 mark for each reason]*.
2 a) 3 marks in total:
  • neat and accurate drawing of jig *[1 mark]*
  • all parts of sketch labelled *[1 mark]*
  • explanation of how to use jig *[1 mark]*
  E.g.

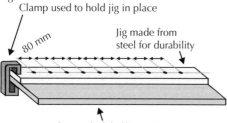

  The jig is placed over the top of the side panel and clamped into place. The holes can then be drilled.
  b) E.g. it can reduce errors / it makes every piece identical / it saves time *[2 marks — 1 mark for each point]*.

Page 60 — Manufacturing in Quantity — 2

3 a) 4 marks in total:
  • full explanation of process *[1 mark]*
  • number of parts to be marked out given *[1 mark]*
  • all materials and tools used *[1 mark]*
  • realistic dimensions for templates given *[1 mark]*
  E.g.

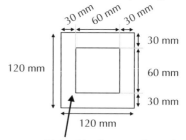

  Make side piece template using stiff card according to dimensions given. Use pencil to draw round template on to the wood 20 times.

  Make base piece template using stiff card. Use pencil to draw round template 5 times.

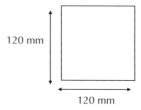

  b) 3 marks in total:
  • instruction to cut around the outside of the side and base pieces *[1 mark]*
  • explanation of how to cut holes in the side pieces *[1 mark]*
  • all materials and tools used given *[1 mark]*
  E.g.

  Use a jigsaw to cut along marked lines for the base and side pieces.

  To cut out the centre pieces of the side panels drill a hole and then use a jigsaw to cut round the lines marked.

Even more brilliant CGP books that might just save your life...

To find out more (or place an order with fantastic next-day delivery),
just visit our website or give our friendly team a call:

www.cgpbooks.co.uk • 0800 1712 712

And of course, our books are available from all good booksellers, including:

ISBN 978 1 84762 398 0

TRAA41